Things that Make You Go Oooommmmm

Insights, prayers, aphorisms,
epiphanies and advice
for myself and other friends

By the author of

Spirituality For Dummies
Secrets of Spiritual Happiness
A Modern Quest for Eternal Truth

Sharon Janis

Night Lotus Books

OM

Oooommmmm

Oooommmmmm

Oooommmmmm

Things that Make You Go Oooommmmm

(Pronounced as the Sanskrit syllable OM or AUM)

Sharon "Kumuda" Janis

Namaste

Things that Make You Go Oooommmmm is a collection of contemplative poetic insights that arose in my mind, heart, and soul during decades of personal exploration in spirituality, science, psychology, and metaphysics.

While producing and editing television shows in Hollywood in the mid-1990s, health issues brought the possibility that my time on earth might be coming to an end.

Sitting quietly for many months, I felt grateful for having enjoyed an interesting, educational, and blessed life, and was at peace with the possibility of passing over to whatever was or was not going to be next.

In the midst of this peaceful repose, I "heard" and sensed an unexpected, soul-stirring message of guidance. This inner command came with a bird's eye view of the eclectic paths of my life journey that had included growing up with psychology teachers and many years of close study with spiritual masters.

If I were to translate this inner guidance into audible voice, would describe the message as being delivered with a "voice of God" flavor that reminded me of the burning bush scene from the *Ten Commandments* movie, where God tells Moses, "Put off thy shoes from off thy feet, for the place thou standest is holy ground."

The command I received was:

"First, you have to share
what you've learned."

After receiving this message, I wrote books, including *Spirituality For Dummies*, *Secrets of Spiritual Happiness*, and *A Modern Quest for Eternal Truth*, recorded audio recitations of spiritual poetry and scriptures, including the "Diamond Sutra" and "Bhagavad Gita" sung in English, and produced many charitable, spiritual, and documentary films. These contemplations are offered in the same spirit of inspired service.

Blessings on your path!

OM

Oooommmmm

Oooommmmm

Oooommmmm

One secret of immortality
is to realize that the
"You" you *thought* was you
never truly existed.

Oooommmmm

It's more important for everything
to be done at the right moment
than to be done more quickly.

Oooommmmm

Instead of looking for
someone to "complete you,"
complete yourself, and then
find those who complement you.

Oooommmmm

Be less selfish,
and more Self-ish.

Oooommmmm

Before you can take a breath,
first you must give a breath.

Such are the cycles
of giving and receiving.

Oooommmmm

Just because something
could be done,
or even *should* be done,
doesn't mean it is *your*
assigned job to do it.

Oooommmmm

Always strive to be
more helpful than harmful.

Oooommmmm

If you don't like it, change it.
And if you don't change it, like it.

Oooommmmm

There's nowhere to go,
and nothing to do.

It's all happening inside of you.

Everyone is on a spiritual journey.

It's just that some are striving
to do it consciously.

We have to be ready
to go from this world, at any moment.
Then we can live with greater freedom.

Ask yourself, every now and then,
"Am I ready to go right now?"

Practice letting go of this world
before this world lets go of you.

If you think you are the body,
then when the body dies,
you, in a sense, also die.

If you identify with That
which is beyond the body,
when the body dies,
your consciousness remains.

Oooommmmm

Find the deep calling of your soul.

God puts deep in your heart
what you're supposed to do,
and what you're supposed to
give to this world.

Oooommmmm

O Supreme Soul,
Grant me the grace to break free
from the illusion-bound one who is asking.

Oooommmmm

Life is a reality show;
Life is THE reality show.

Look at life as a play, and enjoy the show!

Ooommmm

Ultimately, our loyalty can only be
for the greatest good.

Ooommmm

Every moment of the
dance of your life is meaningful.

Every person you encounter in any way at all
has an important movement
in your dance.

Ooommmm

There is no punishment,
only guidance.

Ooommmm

Don't worry too much about
pushing things you don't resonate with.

Focus more on what does resonate.

Oooommmmm

If it doesn't flow, don't go.

Don't do what doesn't feel right,
unless you have to.

Oooommmmm

Don't depend on
other people to define you.

Oooommmmm

Who writes the dream?

If you want to expand your awareness
of who you really are,
simply ask yourself:
"Who writes the dream?"

Oooommmmm

Who is the "Thy,"
in "Thy will be done?"

Oooommmmm

Relish each day,
and at the same time, let go.

Oooommmmm

In a sense, all words are mantras.

Specific patterns of word sounds have specific effects on our bodies, minds, hearts, atmosphere, and experience.

Oooommmmm

When you realize how powerful words are,
you tend to become much more careful
about how you speak,
even in the smallest situations.

Oooommmmm

"Good Morning" is a natural affirmation
we have created to declare the morning good,
to affirm a positive intention
at the beginning of each day.

It's a western version of a mantra.

Oooommmmmm

I don't relate to people's roles.
I relate to their souls.

Oooommmmmm

When you become freer from greed,
you don't act nice to someone
only because they gave you something
or did something nice for you,
or because they could give you something
or do something nice for you.

Everyone is inherently precious
and worthy of kindness and respect.

Oooommmmmm

It is said that Man is made
in the image and likeness of God.

We think that means God looks like us;
what it means is that
we really look like "Him,"
beyond the veil of appearances.

Oooommmm

This lifetime is but a drop in the
ocean of Consciousness; just one step
of a long, eternal, timeless journey.

Oooommmm

Onward, upward, forward, happy.

Oooommmm

It's the moments of deeper meaning,
fuller feeling, and inner transformation
that are most important.

Oooommmm

Everything we've experienced comes together
for whatever we're being called to do.

Oooommmmm

Step by step, veil by veil,
stop hiding your glory.

Oooommmmm

This is your life, your responsibility,
and your gift. Use it, or lose it.

Oooommmmm

When you reach a certain point,
anything you do is *seva*, selfless service,
and everything you give is a tithe.

Oooommmmm

Remember that it's all temporary.

Oooommmmm

In that higher space,
the "physical" realm is no longer the priority.

It's just one of many things
going on at the same time.

Ooo0mmmm

Most important, perhaps,
is the evolutionary step we're to take
as human incarnations on this earth plane.

Ooo0mmmm

"I AM" is the way.

Ooo0mmmm

There are so many states of consciousness
within our own beings,
of which we have no knowledge.

Yet we think our waking state
must be the most important.

Ooo0mmmm

This world is made up of
the substance of illusion.
Everything we think is subject to
the distorting and ever creative mind.

Oooommmmm

Renunciation brings freedom.

Oooommmmm

Sometimes things go better if we can trust the nature-intelligence and stay out of the way.

Oooommmmm

Take moments in your day to listen to sounds.

Conscious listening is a form of meditation that focuses the mind, stretches sensory awareness mechanisms, and brings a calming of the many frivolous and seemingly important thoughts that fly through our mental framework — not just once, but over and over again, day after day.

Oooommmmm

Don't limit
where wisdom comes from,
or through whom God speaks to you.

Oooommmmm

We study and serve and work,
and contemplate and philosophize and love,
and feel and give and receive and care,
and try and trust and respect,
all while knowing that it is all
(as far as we can know)
ultimately meaningless.

Oooommmmm

How would you behave
if you knew you were going to die?

Ok, now behave that way,
Because guess what?

You are.

Oooommmmm

When asked whether
I believe in reincarnation,
the question doesn't quite apply
to my deeper belief system.

My belief is more that infinite universes
are created and destroyed in each moment,
and that everything projects
into time, space, presence, and form,
like holographic images,
from the formless, Eternal Now.

Oooommmmm

It's not about how much
hardship or ease you have in life.

It's about who you are,
wherever you are.

Oooommmmm

Trust the bigger picture.

Oooommmmm

In the state of transcendence,
both the pleasant and unpleasant
are merely two flavors of Universal Bliss.

When something happens, instead of looking
only for an outer cause, look also at
the inner, karmic, and grace causes:

Inner: How you may have participated in
creating the situation.

Karmic: What it is teaching or
bringing into balance?

Grace: Blessings are hidden in every event.

That sublime space of Consciousness is who I
really am, and not the images
I project into the world.

Dear God – make me whatever
you want me to be, but make it good.

I say this to God,
and God says the same to me:
"Make ME whatever YOU want me to be,
but make it good." Aha!

Oooommmmm

Spirituality is a sense and remembrance
of one's connection with the Divine.

Oooommmmm

If there's one thing that doesn't deserve
to be put into the box of human
mental convenience, it's God.

Oooommmmm

GOD:
Generous Omniscient Divinity

Oooommmmm

God puts deep in our hearts what we're supposed to do and what we're supposed to receive from and give to this world — whether big or small, famous or publicly unknown, loved or feared, leader or follower, or any combination of all these and more.

Our job is to find that
deep inner calling of our soul
beneath all the cacophony
of outer experiences.

The connection with God:
When you don't feel it, you trust it.

One eye open to the world,
one eye focused on God;
the two together
create the vision of a mystic.

I want God to guide my steps.

In fact, I insist on it.

Oooommmmm

If I'm talking to a Christian, I call it Jesus.

If I'm talking to a Taoist, I call it the Tao.

If I'm talking to a worshipper
of the Divine Mother, I say "Jai Maa."

At other times, it is my Guru,
the inner Self, or Supreme Consciousness.

Oooommmmm

One secret is that we get what we hope for,
AND we get what we fear.

Oooommmmm

Don't just read books, read life.

Oooommmmm

<blockquote>
Becoming realized can be like
putting up Christmas lights.
</blockquote>

First, you spend a lot of time setting up the right designs and patterns of the strands of light.

Only then, with the flick of a switch, do you turn it on and see, at once, the glory of all you have created.

Life is like this also — every action and thought is another strand being set in place.

<blockquote>
One day, when the lights come on,
you will see the breathtaking glory of
all you have knowingly or unknowingly
created and always been.
</blockquote>

Oooommmmm

It's not that there's only one enlightenment.

Every person has their own unique experience of enlightenment, and also their own unique path and journey toward enlightenment.

Oooommmmm

You don't have to be perfect,
because you are amazing.

Oooommmmm

At some point,
I started to really be happy
to see great things happen to people.

There wasn't that throb of jealousy or insecurity that may have once accompanied the positive feelings when witnessing someone's good fortune.

Instead, there is a pure sense of joy and happiness at seeing our beneficent universe do its thing.

Oooommmmm

When you die,
this entire world slides off of you
like a snake shedding its skin.

Oooommmmm

The important part about
learning higher truths
is to transform learned information
and objective understanding
into subjective experience.

Book knowledge is not enough.

Ooooommmm

A little mistake here and there
can be good for the soul.

Having to admit mistakes or redo things
teaches patience and humility.

Ooooommmm

Humility lets you see your mistakes
and make positive changes, without shame.

Ooooommmm

It's okay to think things without saying them.

Ooooommmm

From a day-to-day life perspective,
we make disappointing mistakes,
but from the universal view,
all Is Perfection.

Oooommmmm

Realize the power inherent in your own words, in the syllables that pass over your tongue and through your lips.

This is one gift of being a human being.

Oooommmmm

Communication happens
on countless levels,
through every interaction
that takes place in this creation.

Oooommmmm

True sacrifices don't feel like sacrifices.

Oooommmmm

How soon do you think you will
be ready to receive the abundance
of realization, joy, love and wealth
that is waiting to come into your life?

My spiritual practice
is to do what I'm guided to do,
when I'm guided to do it.

The element of Time
blinds us to our true nature.

If the element of time is taken out of the picture, we are all the one eternal being that is omniscient and omnipresent.

Anything is possible.

Instead of always trying
to fulfill countless desires,
learn to like what is good for you.

Oooommmmm

It's amazing how nice and tolerant people
can get when troubles come their way.

Learn to be nice and tolerant
without the troubles,
and you'll save yourself
a lot of troubles.

Oooommmmm

Being useful
keeps us youthful.

Oooommmmm

It is not that karmas are there to punish,
but to teach.

Oooommmmm

The maps through which we view reality
are like cages within a dream.

Try as we may to blast, cut, or
push them open, all we really have to do
is wake up from this dream of the world,
and realize that those cages
never even existed.

May the one
who awakens from this dream
feel refreshed.

Living in the monastic ashram, I learned to surrender to time and, in a sense, transcend time. Days felt like years, and years felt like days. Time became secondary to the flow. All winters were one winter, more connected by the quality of being winter than by linear time.

Spiritual attainment is not as much
about being smart or skilled,
as it is about being guided.

Of course, being smart and skilled
can help with understanding and
acting on the guidance.

Oooommmmm

My prayers always end with:
In the right place, at the right time,
in the right way, and "obo"
(or best offer).

I Always give Universal Consciousness
a line item veto for any details I may try
to slip onto the deeper core issue prayer.

Oooommmmm

God's will be done;
my suggestions be considered.

Oooommmmm

Things don't come when you're needy.
Stop being needy!!!

Ooommmm

So help me God.

So, help me God.

So help me, God.

Ooommmm

The idea is to experience your life
on spiritual and world levels
at the same time, together.

Ooommmm

Many of the yogic practices followed
by ancient Indian seekers of truth
are for the purpose of closing up
spigot holes that waste our precious energies.

Ooommmm

The universe is perfect.
That doesn't mean it is always nice.

Oooommmmm

If you feel friction from an action, that may sometimes mean it is not the right thing to do or the best time to do it.

Although, sometimes that friction is helping to strengthen and prepare you to do the action.

Look beyond outer frictions for the friction-free Tao, the Way, the Flow, the divine energy that is free of friction even in the midst of frictions.

Oooommmmm

Do your best, and surrender the rest.

Oooommmmm

Prayer and affirmation:
Everything at the right time,
in the perfect way.

Oooommmmm

Either you trust God, or you don't.
I choose to trust.

Oooommmm

We can always trust God.

The question is whether
God can always trust us,
and if we can always trust ourselves.

Oooommmm

A drop of sincere gratitude
is much more valuable
than a great deal of forced gratitude,
or surface gratitude.

Oooommmm

Intentionally create a habit of gratitude.
We already have so many habits.
Choose gratitude as a habit.

Oooommmm

Understand that you have inherent value,
regardless of what you do or don't have
in the material world.

Ooommmmm

Time is more precious than money.

Even the wealthiest human beings
long to buy more time.

Ooommmmm

Every one is wealthy in something.

What are you wealthy in?

Ooommmmm

There is no one in this world
who compares with the relationship
to God, to the Universe,
to the Supreme Self.

Ooommmmm

When we're in an expanded point of view,
it is impossible to experience boredom.

Nothing in existence or non-existence
can possibly be boring; it's all magnificent,
down to the hypothetical smallest particle.

Oooommmmm

Grace can come
unbidden and unexpectedly,
And once the hand of Grace is felt,
one's entire being is transfigured —
even if the tangible effects of that blessing
may become more visible in the future.

Oooommmmm

Life is a creative project.

Oooommmmm

More than a face lift, we need an attitude lift.

Oooommmmm

Everything in my life is in God's Hands:
The Good, the Good, and the Good.

Why create Bad and Ugly? It's all good!

Oooommmmm

I welcome you into my life,
and I also welcome you out of my life,
should that time come.

Oooommmmm

There's the experience, and then there's
the attempt to put that experience into words.

Sometimes putting an experience into words can enhance our remembrance and understanding, giving a chance to milk potent moments for more growth and blessings.

At the same time, the words are still just a map representing an experience that the mind could only partially perceive.

Oooommmmm

Life is multi-leveled;
each event can be viewed on many levels.

An artist's or sage's expression
of their profound experience can
open the door for countless others
to experience some measure
of that original experience,
in their own way.

Sometimes it is not a matter
of who could do something best,
but of who actually does it.

The idea that there is
no other life in the universe
is just the silliest thing… in the universe.

Karma isn't about retribution,
it's about learning and growing,
and going deeper and deeper
into the meaning of existence —
discovering more and more about
the flow and divine laws of nature.

Oooommmmm

If we tear off the false labels
of "good" or "bad,"
there is power in any intense experience,
and also in any peaceful, quiet experience.
With focus and grace, any experience can give
entrance into deeper and greater realms.

Oooommmmm

We are a work in progress
that is already done.

Oooommmmm

May the world awaken to greater Truth.

Oooommmmm

"God" first,
everything else next.

What do we look for in the events of our lives? Are we grateful for the lessons and spiritual breakthroughs in our consciousness?

We feel happy when accomplishing things that are considered "important," but those may only be important in terms of the illusive structure of cultural hierarchy into which each person has been born.

What about the importance of
subtle, profound moments?

What about deeper events that often occur during life's most seemingly mundane moments?

Do without doing.

There's the higher self and the lower self.
The higher self understands,
while the lower self experiences.

Oooommmmm

Photographing nature is a dance with God.

Oooommmmm

Mother nature gave us the ability to whistle
so we could talk with the birds.

Oooommmmm

We can know nothing as intimately as our own experience: our minds, bodies, the dreams we have at night, deep urges, emotions, inspirations that sweep through our being, hopes we carry, the goodness that is our essence, the confusion we feel, and the insights we catch.

Even insights about external phenomena
can be understood through internal reflection.

Oooommmmm

My Guru used to chuckle as
he spoke of the millions of dollars
we had spent to send a ship to the moon.

He would travel through
infinite realms, dimensions and worlds
just by closing his eyes and
entering the inner space.

Ooooommmmm

Philosophy is a skill like any other.

Some may be predisposed to have the talent,
but practice also plays a role.

Ooooommmmm

Grace will find dreams
you didn't even know you had,
or didn't dare believe could be possible,
and will bring them into your life,
naturally and easefully.

Ooooommmmm

Part of what's tricky about Grace
manifesting our deepest desires outwardly
is that sometimes what we think we want
isn't what we really want
on other levels of our being.

Oooommmmm

Look for opportunities to pray.
Prayers are like e-mail to God.

Oooommmmm

Have you talked with your Universe today?

Oooommmmm

    Being enlightened is like being an actor and knowing that all the scenes are just dramas for entertainment. Life is like a big drama, and those who remember that they're actors in a play get to wink at one another from behind the scenery.

Oooommmmm

Some things are too precious to be sold.
They must be given.

Ooooommmmm

Sitting quietly helps to break the hypnotic trance of the world, and gives us an opportunity to expand our subjective experience.

While sitting, we begin to feel our own energies. We begin to watch the activities of our mind, and experience ourselves standing as the witness of our own mental processes.

Through this experience comes the understanding that we are not our mind.

We are the One who thinks through the mind.

Ooooommmmm

If we get subtle, we can hear into sounds.
There are so many layers of sound,
even in silence.

Ooooommmmm

Stop being just the spoon.

Be the person who prepared the pudding,
be the Divine Mother cook
who delights in tasting Her creation.

Oooommmmm

Cream rises to the top,
no matter how sweet or bitter the brew.

Oooommmmm

In quantum mechanics terms,
one's personality is both
a particle and a wave,
a specific entity and a multidimensional wave
of Supreme Consciousness
within the inestimable ocean of life.

Oooommmmm

It's all God's play.

Oooommmmm

Look at everything
as an opportunity to interact with God.

Oooommmmm

We can't help everybody in the world,
but we can help someone.

Oooommmmm

When our karma furnaces aren't being stuffed constantly with countless actions, and more importantly, with constant interpretations of actions, such as, "I did this great thing," or, "I shouldn't have said that," then there is a chance to begin to burn the stored karmas that hold us down just as surely as a couple of big stomach rolls.

Oooommmmm

Speaking of stomach rolls,
I'd rather be fat and enlightened
than not fat and not enlightened.

Oooommmmm

Realize that you are divinity,
Universal Consciousness, pure spirit,
God Himself and Herself
playing the roles you play
in and as your entire life,
and the roles of everyone else too.

This realization naturally transforms
and uplifts every element of our life,
including the work we do and our attitude
that goes into every action we perform.

Oooommmmm

If you know it is God who has
slapped you on one cheek,
of course you would then
offer the other cheek.

Oooommmmm

Grace in every step;
happy to stay, ready to go.

Oooommmmm

It takes Oneness to know Oneness.

It's no accident that God made our arms
flexible enough to hug ourselves.

One way to measure our progress
toward inner freedom
is to see how much we have broken free
from our sense of egocentricity,
our notion of separateness.

That is more important
than getting more money,
or proving yourself to others.

I love people,
but am not always a fan of the species.

An unaware person lives in a very fast subjective world, missing all kinds of time and details while skidding unconsciously through life.

The artist pauses to notice colors and appreciate the play of light and shadow on whatever scene is before their eyes.

Musicians can expand time and fill it with melodies, harmonies, rhythms and various patterns of sound intertwined with one another, reflecting the grand universal symphony.

Oooommmmm

Everything is alive.

Oooommmmm

It's always easy
and I'm always blessed.

God's grace is with me;
I release the rest.

Oooommmmm

The practices of meditation
and inward reflection
keep our energies from flowing out
as strongly through the senses,
which are always looking for pleasure
in external experiences.

Ooommmm

Take a *real* Selfie,
with the camera of meditation.

Ooommmm

All experience is actually memory.

Even "present time" experience is
a split-second memory playback
through the interpretive and image storage
capacities of the brain and mind.

Ooommmm

It's all intricately designed.

Ooommmm

No concept of God, the universe, or anything else a human mind can possibly conceive of is anywhere near one particle of THAT light of ultimate, unknowable Truth.

It is nonsensical to even postulate percentages about this.

Oooommmmm

When you meditate, you begin to see your thoughts. When you see your thoughts, you realize that you are not your thoughts or the mind that is thinking them, but rather you are the witness, the watcher, the pure awareness-consciousness that exists far beyond the mind and the worlds it creates.

Oooommmmm

Once you realize and understand what you are and what you aren't, then you don't have to feel bad for not being what you are not.

Oooommmmm

Just because someone has
cool things to say or share,
doesn't mean they are always right.
Just because someone can walk on water,
doesn't mean they are free from faults.

Knowing that God exists in everyone is like the difference between someone who sees the sun go down and thinks, "Oh, the sun is going down, I'd better bring in the animals," and another who stops to relish and experience the glory of the Divine Artist's beautiful sunset.

The practice of
independent contentment
keeps us from mulling
over and over in our minds
all the desires, successes
and failures we have experienced.

With every challenge, there's a choice between heaven and hell:

Faith = Heaven
Worry = Hell

Oooommmmm

Each of us is a spark of the eternal, great, soul that exists beyond time — the "Before Abraham was, I Am" aspect of all creation.

Yet, we are also people who apparently exist in time and space, with all that entails.

Oooommmmm

The spiritual journey takes place between two aspects of ourselves — the little petty guy who is concerned about many things that are not so important in the grand scheme of things, and the eternal, great soul who is the *source* of the whole grand scheme of things.

And what a journey it is!

Oooommmmm

I'm comfortable with the mystery

Oooommmmm

When I'm filled with Grace,
everything I do becomes a spiritual practice.

Oooommmmm

Most people put so much energy into day-to-day concerns — personal interactions, job security, relationships, our houses, cars, dogs, children, financial situations, vacation plans, our next meal, desire for recognition, our weight, our hair style, the hair style of the person sitting next to us, and on and on.

So much of our energy pours out of all these spigots, leaving us depleted for our primary, eternal task of focusing on higher knowledge processes and exploring our inner and outer worlds.

We are explorers, after all.

Oooommmmm

Non-attachment means
that when you're done with something,
you let it go and move on.

Let's say you pick up a book at random and turn to a page that speaks as though it were the lips of the beneficent universe itself giving you just what you need to know for the exact life challenges, road twists and shifts ahead.

With non-attachment, you don't have to feel obliged to spend the next twenty years reading that same book over and over again, without fresh interest or guidance to do so.

Non-attachment allows the universal grace energy to present itself to us in a more efficient, pleasing, or powerful form in every moment.

Oooommmmm

What do you want in life?

Oooommmmm

What do I want?
I want to be the God that I am.

Words can bind us, and words can also make us free — especially if we use enlightened consciousness words that lead us into greater states of conscious awareness, including the thought-free, word-free state.

We can use words
to become free from words.
It's like using one thorn
to pull another thorn from our foot.

Devotional love can naturally
focus our attention on greater goals,
via an image that represents those goals.

I see all the different religions and deities,
including Buddha, Jesus, Allah, and Shiva,
as different flavors of God.

Yum Yum.

Oooommmmm

Chanting and repetition of divine names
puts you on a first name basis with God.

Krishna! Ram! Buddha! Jesus! Shiva!

Hello, it's me!

Oooommmmm

Moods, emotions,
blessings and upheavals
— even death itself —
are but flickers on the screen
of infinite Consciousness
that YOU ARE.

Oooommmmm

    One life lesson can manifest in our lives in many ways at once, like a particularly obvious television script, with interrelating, intertwined events all having to do with different sides of the same topic.

Ooooommmmm

> Every blank piece of paper
> is a potential masterpiece.
>
> Every free moment
> is an opportunity to hug God.

Ooooommmmm

    The *bhakti yoga* practice of focusing one's love and devotion toward an image — a personal manifestation of the divine, allows us to have an experience of divine love, without becoming quite as trapped by the usual kinds of relationship co-dependency issues that often dim our light of love.

Ooooommmmm

If we can be really present
in doing each task life hands to us,
we automatically uplevel
the power that moves
through every moment of our lives.

Oooommmmm

Gratitude is not only for
when good things come to you.
It's a special combination of optimism,
faith, surrender, service, humility, and grace.

Oooommmmm

No guilt, just gratitude.

Oooommmmm

Every inner vision
and every seemingly external object
is a potential boat
across the ocean of delusion.

Oooommmmm

The glass is neither half empty nor half full.
It is completely full of water and air.

This shift of perception and appraisal
is similar to the shift of seeing everything
as *Om puranam adah purnam idam*:
this is perfectly full, and that is perfectly full.

Even if you pour all the water
out of the glass, it is still full.

Ooommmmm

Sometimes you just have to jump in,
though you may know not
where you are headed.

Ooommmmm

When we greet
the check-out clerk at a supermarket,
do we do it with
full respect and attention?

Ooommmmm

Through what form will
Supreme Consciousness
speak to me in this moment?

Oooommmmm

We don't have to be conscious
of our beating heart,
or of the intricate universes of
chemical and electrical interactions
that maintain our physical bodies.

In the same way, we are not conscious
of much of what passes through and around
our awareness on many other physical,
psychological, subtle, alternate, and
super-psychical levels.

Oooommmmm

It's all taking place in the present moment.

Even history is taking place
in the present moment.

Oooommmmm

There's a gift to be unwrapped
in every person.
This doesn't mean you have to
chat with everyone you meet,
although it certainly doesn't mean you can't.

It is the space of inner appreciation
that is important.

The world is filled
with millions and billions of people.

If you happen to be standing next to someone
on a subway for fifteen or twenty minutes
on your way to work one morning,
that person has had to conquer
tremendous statistical odds
to find themselves in your presence.

Don't get mad, get glad.

Think of will power as
a light we can shine into the world,
an energy powerful enough to manifest
the image sent with it.

Oooommmmm

Spiritual practices allow us to focus our will.
Usually we want so many things.
Imagine a list of every big or small desire
you've had since the day you were born.

Our will is all over the place,
refracted into a million fragments.

Oooommmmm

My prayer for many things:
May everything be guided and perfect.

Oooommmmm

Life is an amazing game —
we never know when we'll be taken out.

Oooommmmm

Whatever you are doing,
do it in the moment.

If you are planning what to do the following day or the following year, that is ok too, as long as you are planning consciously and in the moment, and not just replaying a dusty old stack of video tapes in your brain, watching them skip back and forth, over and over, replaying the same lessons, thoughts and complaints, but never moving past them.

Listen to all the sounds around you,
and try to discern the harmonics
and symphony.
Listen to the air, hear the pulsation
of blood rushing by your ears,
try to hear the universal throb,
the one vibration
that underlies the whole shebang.

This entire universe sings the same song.

Oooommmmm

An artist sees beauty
even in how the sunlight falls
on a pile of garbage in the alley.

Oooommmmm

Sometimes the best thing
you can do is nothing.

Oooommmmm

Many elements of western medicine, from radiation diagnostics to pharmaceutical cocktails, cause damage along with the good — in many cases, far more damage than good.

Society at large must also learn how to
eat, live, and manufacture products
that are more naturally healthy.

Oooommmmm

If we have fewer, higher goals, the "light beam" of our will-power energy becomes stronger, like a laser beam in which all the light waves are moving in a highly synchronized pulsation.

> A laser beam is strong enough
> to cut through steel.

> Ooommmmm

> You must be present to win.

> Ooommmmm

To grasp the deeper, more meaning-filled levels beyond our surface lives, we must shift the focus of our consciousness, bringing the limited nature out of focus, and the higher levels into focus.

It's similar to looking at 3D stereoscopic images. There is the surface design, but if we shift our focus in just the right way, an entirely different, seemingly unrelated image springs forth.

> Ooommmmm

Try to feel what it would be like
to be able to bestow blessings.

Practice walking around town for one hour,
imagining that you have the power
to give blessings to anyone you choose.

Do you bless everyone?
Do you bless yourself?

Oooommmmm

If God wants me to help someone,
I don't worry about what
they've done or not done for me.
This kind of "non-bookkeeping" attitude
towards giving brings great freedom
and makes us clearer and better vehicles
for God's grace and God's plan
to flow into the world.

Oooommmmm

Let inevitable things be as they are.

Oooommmmm

Before the final enlightenment,
there is an abyss you have to cross.

It's like Wylie Coyote running after the Road Runner. He's running so fast that he doesn't see the edge of the cliff. The next thing you know, he's running on air.

You can't turn back, you can only look forward — and definitely not down! You must make your faith so strong that you're able to run on air to the other side.

I've been running on air for years!

When everything is going right in the outer world, your mind may feel comfortable and secure, even though that is not necessarily the true security, but may be complacency.

True security is there
even when you're in danger.

I like to look at life
with a more philosophical eye.

Oooommmmm

In-between lifetimes, and even in our current life, beneath the level of our usual awareness, there is a baseline current of "realization," a pure awareness running into our bodies, minds and hearts.

That realization awareness is like the raw energy that comes out from the sockets in our homes, animating whatever is connected to it; giving life, yet remaining separate and free from the forms through which it expresses.

That underlying energy current
is like the THAT in "Thou art THAT."

Oooommmmm

Stop working and start serving.

Oooommmmm

It's *ALL* symbolic!

Clean your room, and you clean your life.

Oooommmm

Devotion allows for
magical events or "miracles"
to take place within our reality system,
without our having to understand
exactly how they occurred.

"Thank you for this blessing,
Beloved God."

Oooommmm

We all know from our experience of the dream state that our idea of clock time is not the only kind of time that is available to us.

Two temporal minutes
can contain dream experiences
that appear to go on for years.

Oooommmm

Think of Universal Consciousness as space
to be explored and traveled through —
infinite, far beyond the greatest
anything we can ever know,
in every direction.

Watch events fall upon the lake of time
like drops of rain.
See how the ripples of events
also proceed them.

Oooommmmm

Those who have had a lot of "past lifetimes" tend to be more multifaceted and eclectic.

They may have been both rulers and servants, been kind-hearted or ruthless, with indulgent lifetimes and monastic lifetimes, and having gained expertise in many areas of activities, including child rearing, tilling the fields, cooking, military, writing, dancing, debating, music, merchanting — so many experiences from different lifetimes.

Oooommmmm

Human beings have certainly had
an interesting run of it.

Greed is what most often keeps a person
from having good timing —
also impatience,
which usually stems from greed.

My job is to have faith and trust
that everything is happening
in the right way, and at the right time.

Ultimately, you either have faith in the world,
or you have faith in God.

And if you have true faith in God,
then you can also have faith in the world
as an expression of God.

Perhaps, a future evolutionary step will be for human intelligence and consciousness to become externalized completely from its dependence on the human body, like a computer-based species.

Then, through pollution, plagues,
or other natural and manmade perils,
the human species may die off,
yet its intelligence spirit could live on.

Oooommmmm

True knowledge is ruthless.

Oooommmmm

What you put into your subconscious mind comes out in other parts of your life and speech in various visible and subliminal ways.

If your autocorrect changes *pens* into *penis*, maybe that's something you've typed before.

And so it is with subconscious memory.

Oooommmmm

Don't expect things to be what they're not,
or you'll be disappointed.

When we talk about listening to your heart,
or following your heart,
it's not your physical heart,
but the portion of your being
where your brain and mind intersect
with your wisdom and soul.

Find what is good in every situation.
Focus on the good, and learn from it.
Surrender to whatever gift
a situation is bringing,
even if that gift is to make you
less attached to ephemeral things
so you can strengthen your focus
and communion with spirit.

Try to sit completely still
for an entire hour.
Don't move a muscle!

Oooommmmm

Be excellent
when nobody is watching you.

Oooommmmm

One stage of enlightenment is that
you're looking at things from one side,
contemplating teachings and concepts
with your mind — and suddenly,

Pop!

You're seeing the same things
from the other side.

Oooommmmm

Live according to YOUR nature.

Oooommmmm

Listen for laughter around you.
Jump into other people's laughter,
and your own.
Laughter is a porthole to divine joy.

The fact that it may be my karma to go through certain challenges doesn't necessarily absolve people who contributed to creating those challenges in improper or unkind ways from the karmic fruits of their actions. But that's how the whole game continues.

Karma is the fuel of life experience.

God first, everything else next.

My discipline is: God?
What do you want me to do right now?

We can think of supreme Consciousness, for analogy sake, as an immense ocean, vast and teeming with untold legions of life.

Upon the surface of this ocean is the play of waves. Surfers appear and look for the height and break of each wave. They keep track of the tides and locations of the biggest and best waves for what they do — "surfing."

This analogy also relates to the waves of life, those continual waves of object appearances and disappearances that we all know so well.

Though we may sometimes focus on surface movements, the ocean of Consciousness remains unaffected by the nature of its own waves.

Oooommmmm

Religion is being outwardly guided,
while spirituality is being inwardly guided.

Oooommmmm

A church or house of worship
is only as good as how much
it inspires and creates an atmosphere
for you to talk with God.

You can tell who really "believes in God" by how they respond during times of challenge and crisis — both personal and world crises.

If you're the head of a church, and when things go wrong, you start freaking out and worrying about everything, then you may not fully believe in God.

If you call yourself an atheist, but when the plane hits your office building, you calmly call your wife to tell her you love her, then you may really believe in God.

Everything is up to what we do with it.

Each of us is a spark of the eternal, great, soul that exists beyond time — the "Before Abraham was, I Am" aspect of all creation. Yet, we are also people who apparently exist in time and space, with all that entails.

The entire spiritual journey takes place between these two aspects of ourselves — the little petty guy who is concerned about many things that are not so important in the grand scheme of things, and the eternal, great soul who is the *source* of the whole grand scheme of things.

And what a journey it is!

Oooommmmm

Dear God, grant me the bliss
of complete surrender.
In every moment, may I be prepared to let go of this world and fall into your Loving Arms.

Oooommmmm

There's no "God," because it's all God

Oooommmmm

God gives; I don't have to take.

Our responsibility is what we give to the world in response to whatever experiences are given to us on all the levels that we knowingly or unknowingly interact with the world, including physical, mental, and spiritual.

That's the game.

Right playing of the game brings freedom to be in harmony with Godly, divine vibrations of thought and activity, regardless of what outer events or group think may bring or say to you.

Personality is multi-faceted.
Each facet of our personality
has to become realized.
Every facet has to
awaken to higher Truth.

We move up in layers.

On the spiritual journey,
Layers of "you" burn and die away.

When you feel you can't take
the burning and dissolution anymore,
that is an especially important time
to plant good seeds
for the next phase of your life.

The journey of life
and spiritual evolution
is like a series of mini deaths and rebirths.

Oooommmmm

Life is
the soul's hobby.

Oooommmmm

Don't take things too seriously.

It's just school.

Oooommmmm

The ocean of Consciousness
gives up nothing to create its waves,
nor is it affected by the movements
or particular qualities of its own waves.

And if the waves were to vanish,
yet the ocean would
remain through all,
unaffected.

Ooooommmmm

Some fruits of suffering
for one on the path of self-discovery,
are strength, surrender,
and compassion.

Ooooommmmm

You are more than good enough,
no matter who you are,
or what you or others think you are.

Ooooommmmm

Through an encounter with a great being,
my entire life was completely and
profoundly transformed.

I don't always discuss my feelings about this,
because some might think that I'm just trying to
pitch the particular path that inspired me.

The point is that
this kind of transformation is possible.

Oooommmmm

Sometimes it's necessary
to take someone's hand,
so we can be pulled
out of the quicksand of delusion.

Oooommmmm

Once grace gives you exactly what you need
at the moment enough times,
you start having less worry, and more faith.

Oooommmmm

> "What you are is so loud
> that I can't hear what you are saying."

This is often used as a retort, almost an insult, insinuating that someone is somehow negatively inconsistent with the image they are wishing to present through their words.

Yet this statement reflects an important truth about human nature, interaction, and expression.

Every single thing we do — every movement we make, every word we speak, every piece of clothing we wear — communicates who we are, what we think, and how we feel, to the world around us.

Oooommmmm

> Talk about invasion of privacy!
> We are being watched, revealed,
> and understood on levels
> we've never even dreamed of.

Oooommmmm

There's always an audience.

Oooommmmm

People are concerned about privacy, with surveillance cameras, recorded conversations, and internet hacking, but God, in many visible and invisible forms, is watching each movement of your baby toe.

Forget the paparazzi!

The akashic records are recording every unspoken thought, every spoken word, and every important and unimportant moment of your life. Pass the popcorn.

Oooommmmm

We're the entertainment.

Oooommmmm

Earth is just another electron moving around its nucleus, the sun.

Oooommmmm

Worlds upon worlds
are swirling around with us,
with we planets around our sun.
But we don't see them
through our limited instruments and senses.

We're constantly spinning,
but we don't feel it.
Everything inside ourselves is moving,
but we think we are solid.
When will we integrate
all that we already know?

Everything is many things all at once.

All news is good news
from the biggest picture perspective.

Trust the inner voice —
not the mental drone,
but the throb of life essence
pulsating throughout the atoms
of our experience.

Oooommmmm

The essence of compassion
and non-jealousy
is to realize Oneness.

Good for one is good for all.
Good for you is good for me.

We are reflections
of the same light.

Oooommmmm

Each person's realization is different.

The key is to find
your own realization.

Oooommmmm

Spirituality is
putting first things first.

Make me a flower that
blossoms so beautifully,
and with such
exquisite fragrance,
that even the Supreme Being,
that Consciousness within which
the entire universe as we know it
is a mere speck,
must bend down from
its lofty state to inhale the loving scent.

That sublime space of Consciousness
is who I really am,
and not the images I project
into the world.

The purpose of spirituality, IMHO, is to give a higher perspective, to inspire hope, and to bring a light of grace that lifts us up out of the ever-changing, ephemeral circumstances, and into the eternal light of God.

Oooommmmm

Spirituality doesn't necessarily mean you're
rich, famous, or perfectly healthy;
in fact, it may mean you are
none of those things.

Oooommmmm

In my life, if someone goes against me, even if I feel mad at them, I'll simultaneously make an effort to see them and the entire situation as God's play, God's expression, and the Universal Guru's test and lesson, to give experiential teachings that can make me more spiritually pure and strong — at least in the long run, even if I'm not always feeling so pure and strong in the moment of testing.

Oooommmmm

The real deal can recognize the real deal.

Ooommmm

In some ways, the universe is like a child.
It responds to positive reinforcement.

So send out happy, grateful feelings
and good thoughts about what you want,
and tone down the dramatic excitement
over events and experiences that you don't.

This one step will uplift your life
into greater harmony.

Ooommmm

May my mind,
my subconscious mind,
and the universal mind
all be in harmony
and working together
toward the greatest good.

Ooommmm

It's amazing when
you start to burn old karmas.

It's like when you stop eating too many
calories so your energy system has a chance
to burn the old stored fat.

Oooommmmm

If you let them, things can
appear when you need them.

You don't have to make up a history
to justify their appearance.

Just say thanks.

Oooommmmm

When asked to do something,
my main question is not
how much I would get paid,
but am I *supposed* to do it?

Oooommmmm

Sometimes renunciation
means renouncing our concept
of what renunciation is.

One sign of being in the flow is that everything fits, like when you pour your tea or unmeasured drink into a cup or glass and find that it fits perfectly.

That's a small, symbolic sign
of being in the flow.

"Perfect pour perfection" also comes from your brilliant subconscious mind that can measure everything perfectly, without bothering you about it.

May God bless you
with everything you deserve
in a kindly, forgiving, and loving fashion.

One secret to learning from various teachings, paths, and great beings: You have to be a good editor. Choose and enhance the best nectar-truth-grace-wisdom, and leave the rest, at least for now, on the cutting room floor.

That includes, of course,
what you read in this book.

Oooommmmm

I don't have to know
what I don't have to know,
as long as I know whatever I must know
when I must know it.

This is part of the surrender of serving
and being guided by the hand of God,
acceptance of being on a
need-to-know basis.

Oooommmmm

God and I are on the same team.

Oooommmmm

Why does it seem that the greatest periods of growth in life often follow the most difficult times? We can learn about this phenomenon by watching a father's response when his son falls down while climbing a tree.

The father, in most cases, will pick the son up and console him. He'll hold the child closely and speak in his most soothing tone of voice. Then, perhaps, he'll flip the child in the air to cheer him up, twirling him around magically on his descent back to the ground.

The child, rejuvenated by
all these blessings of love, affection and fun,
will run off happily to climb the next tree.

Oooommmmm

The "Holy Father" essence is
a quality and archetype
of the universe itself,
as, of course, is the Divine Mother.

Oooommmmm

Just as human fathers are a contracted form of the Great Universal Father archetype, so the limited version of human knowledge and mental awareness that we generally live in is distilled from the expanded archetypal level of pure omniscience.

When we see the responses of a father to his child, both in love and in discipline, we can learn more about our own relationship to the Holy Father archetype of God manifesting in and as the Universe.

This is just one of many archetypes through which we interact with the universe.

Oooommmmm

We process experience in many ways at the same time, in time and outside of time and through countless memories, moods, archetypal perceptions, and other aspects of our multi-faceted beings.

Oooommmmm

It doesn't matter what you have
in your bank account.
It matters what you have
in Consciousness.

Oooommmmm

Dear Lord, Fulfill my highest aspirations,
and release any lower ones
in a harmless, appropriate way.

Oooommmmm

It's not only that we see in others
what we ourselves are;
we also become that which we focus on.
It's all one big feedback loop.

Oooommmmm

I am so powerful,
and I'm absolutely nothing.

Oooommmmm

I give my heart's full intention
to God's Glory expressing
fully and beautifully as my life.

Oooommmmm

Sometimes reflected light
is more tangible than the source.

For example, there is bright sunlight, but the reflection of that sunlight on the glistening waves of the ocean can be even more blinding than the sun itself.

The love of the Supreme Soul is infinite, yet we don't always experience it. We may seek a more tangible love in relationship with another person, who is a human reflection of the infinite, Supreme Soul.

Similarly, Divine Grace is eternally present, but we may need the form of a holy one to allow us to drink of it.

Oooommmmm

Guided by God,
inspired by the Guru,
Powered by Grace.

One reason for a seeker to go to a spiritual guru is because you need someone to help pull you out of certain ruts. We all do.

Just as you can't tickle yourself, there are some avenues of healing and growth that may require a guru, in one of many forms through which the Universal Guru may express.

When Jesus said "I am the Way," it's like how you have to go through the secretary to get to the CEO or president of a corporation.

I learned this lesson in Hollywood:
Always be nice to the secretary!

Part of what we have to sort out
is how to discern what is best for us
amid the clamor and clatter of a world
that is trying to tell us what we should want,
and who we should be.

Oooommmmm

One mentality of recent decades was,
"We can exploit people and make money."

The mentality of the future, if we are to survive and thrive, will look more like various levels and versions of:

We are here to live beautiful, fun, kind, and fruitful lives of mutual bounty, in peace and acceptance, with an awareness of the greater journey and journeys of life, with individuals, corporations, and the government making choices for the greater good, the good of all.

Obviously, it will require a paradigm shift,
but anything is possible in this
Field of Consciousness.

Oooommmmm

The ancient knowledge was great,
but the ancient knowledge
combined with all of our
present knowledge and information
would be explosive and spectacular.

Some "spiritual people" use spiritual wisdom
primarily to convince you to buy things
you probably don't need.

Sometimes "spiritual people" can be
the least spiritual people.

Almost everyone looks better
when you don't see them too closely.

Money can't protect you nearly as much
as true, strong faith can.

I am not afraid of anything.
I am not in competition with anyone.
I trust in God completely.

Signed, Me.

Oooommmmm

Be God Awe-Full
in a good way!

Full of awe for the divine.

Oooommmmm

Things can get tough as we are
breaking through to new personal vistas,
because as old patterns and traumas
leave our psychophysical system,
they can brush by our experience
with their toxic flavor.

In some cases, we're feeling it
because it's coming out.

Oooommmmm

Dreams are clues
given to show us
what this universe is made of.

Oooommmmm

Dreams serve many purposes,
including as a karmic discharge.

Along with many other functions,
dreams are image and feeling based
processing and releases of karmic energies.

Oooommmmm

It is through dreams that helpers
on various planes and dimensions
can give blessings or lessons more easily.

Sometimes they'll help train our
unconscious and subconscious layers of mind
on a matter that will be coming up
so we will be better prepared to respond
in a more positive and fruitful way.

Oooommmmm

Being great doesn't mean someone has no human frailties or imperfect tendencies.

Although vigilance is important,
one challenge for humanity
is a tendency to tear down
what is most important.

Oooommmmm

A spiritual person shouldn't have to completely curtail his or her own life and spiritual journey just to teach and give blessings to people who may have limited expectations of what is right and wrong for a spiritual person to do.

One reporter was surprised
when I drank coffee!

Oooommmmm

Less motive,
more guidance.

Oooommmmm

You are a passenger on this trip of life.

Not only are you *a* passenger,
but THE passenger.

Oooommmmm

Whatever God gives,
accept it,
deal with it,
and allow yourself to enjoy it.

Oooommmmm

"World wide web" devices
are training humanity
to interact with the astral plane,
beyond time and space.

Oooommmmm

I want to have exactly how much money
I'm supposed to have.

Oooommmmm

At some point, my prayer became,

"Please keep me free from that which would
distract me from moving with the Tao,
the flow of perfection
that is the nature of life.
Don't distract my journey
with concerns about money
and petty relationships.
Keep me simple. keep me free."

Oooommmmm

You can be humble
and still know you're great.

Oooommmmm

The trick is to increase self-respect
without increasing limited ego.

Oooommmmm

When you're not selling, you can be honest.

Oooommmmm

My Guru began his lectures
by welcoming everyone with
great respect and love, and all his heart.

Greet everything and everyone in your life
with this inner intention,
and your whole life
will transform in a great way.

Oooommmm

Through the study of art,
we learn to appreciate
the power of light, darkness and colors.

If we study psychology, we'll be able to dissect
the hidden inner motivations of
those around us,
and perhaps even ourselves.

If we study miracles, we'll find them.

if we study pain and suffering, we'll have
more opportunities to grow from them.

Oooommmm

Un-integrated, unpracticed knowledge
is nearly as useless as ignorance.

Oooommmmm

Often with events of life,
the lessons to be learned,
and the karmas to be experienced
are more important than what appears
to be going on in the surface layer of things.

Oooommmmm

I pray that my service to humanity
be anointed in every moment,
and at every step, with the glory of
God's blessing, and with my full obedience
to His Will and the higher Goodness of life.

Oooommmmm

Anything is possible.

Oooommmmm

Once you're okay about dying,
everything else becomes easier

Oooommmmm

We all know the death of the body is inevitable, but we don't really know what will happen after the body dies — if the soul lives on in other planes, or returns for another go at it, or if the soul energy simply merges back into the undifferentiated universal energy.

One day we will know, but by then,
we will be a different *we* than we are now.

Oooommmmm

Part of the game of life
is to become immortal before we die.

Wherever we are right now,
with all our circumstances,
that is our starting point.

Oooommmmm

Everything in the outer world may ultimately be "busy work," like what a teacher gave you in school when she was waiting for the right day to begin the next lesson.

Our job may be to enjoy the busy work while remaining attentive and ready to drop it all when God calls – whether through "body death," or by stopping to meditate, or in the midst of a crisis that breaks the veil of worldly illusory complacency for a time.

Learn to drop it all before *it* drops you.

Oooommmmm

Before you can become free from death,
you first have to go through
your fear and distaste with death.

Oooommmmm

I want to have a wonderful and
very cool death, when the time comes.

Oooommmmm

Turn fear of losing
into gratitude for having

Oooommmm

After this life, we receive reflections
of how we lived here.
Some have described these reflections
as worlds of heaven or hell.

Oooommmm

Have gratitude and appreciation for
people around you —
even those you pass on the street or in a store.

Don't wait for a disaster to make you
appreciate one another.

Oooommmm

If you can be grateful
for even your hardships,
you're doing pretty good.

Oooommmm

The essence of spirituality
is to experience divinity
within and without.

Oooommmmm

If we can gain the same faith in THAT, which manufactured this universe, as we have in the rollercoaster's engineer, then we get to enjoy the ups and downs of life as a fun ride.

With faith in the rollercoaster's engineer, fear becomes excitement, as we enjoy even the scary drops, without being taken over by a painful form of fear.

We see ourselves going up and up and up, and then we stop, overlooking a cliff that seems to go straight down, to our doom, certain death, impossible to survive. Yet we know deep inside that we will be safe and sound by the end of the ride.

This is what faith in God is like.

Oooommmmm

The "I" can't get no satisfaction,
Give up the "I."

We have to find the essence of all traditions,
the light behind the projection,
the object to which
the shadow of this world alludes.

I'm just here to study the species.

We can practice virtues
no matter where we are.

Even in the worst circumstances
such as in concentration camps,
virtuous souls continued to shine
like flames in the darkness.

To love without attachment...

What an amazing goal to strive for
and to achieve.

Love in the moment,
with no mental, emotional,
or other limiting tendrils
into past or future.

Oooommmmm

God judges you
according to how you judge.

When do you give your pets treats? Do you make them do tricks first, or are they inherently worthy of receiving treats just by virtue of being your pet? Do you want God to make you do tricks for grace, or to give grace freely, simply because you belong to God.

Rumi said "The way you love
is the way God will be with you."

Oooommmmm

Ultimately there is no blame,
and no personal responsibility
separate from the Supreme Will
that creates, sustains, and
forever moves through
every single atom, object,
and activity in this manifestation.

Oooommmm

We're each responsible
for our state of well being,
and for how we can help each other.

Oooommmm

Many think that when you say someone lives by their own rules, it means they want to get away with more unacceptable behavior.

But in spiritual cases, living by your own rules often means imposing stricter rules on yourself than most of society does, at least in certain respects.

Oooommmm

Life and death also take place within one life.

Sometimes layers of "you" burn and die away, like layers of an onion peeling off.

When you feel you can't take it anymore or you feel like something inside yourself is dying, that is the time to use your best consciousness to plant the seed of your future "birth" or "life" within your life, like a mini- death and rebirth.

The Indian scriptures say that whatever we think of at the moment of death determines where we go next. It's the same with these mini-deaths we experience during life.

Stay especially vigilant during difficult times!

Oooommmmm

Money often makes us create karma.
Good karma, bad karma,
helping, ignoring, choosing, giving,
misgiving, blessing, harming, and so on.

Oooommmmm

The human race is like a mediocre student who moves through school, not necessarily building upon all the knowledge he has learned, but forgetting most of the insights and lessons from one class as he moves to the next.

    Imagine what the ancient Egyptians must have understood.

Oooommmmm

When I hear some spiritual teachers suggest dropping or forgetting your past, I feel that would be like throwing away a meal before you've finished eating.

    It can be especially helpful to remember powerful and significant moments, and also to share them as guided.

Oooommmmm

    We've done this all before.

Oooommmmm

Greater growth is not just about
getting more knowledge,
or doing more things,
but about meeting the
right knowledge at the right time,
doing the right things at the right times,
and being in harmony with the
universal pattern of each moment.

Oooommmmm

What some call wishful thinking,
I call visioning.

Oooommmmm

Some people think that if they prepare
for something, that means it won't happen.

Others think that if they *don't* prepare
for something, that means it won't happen.

Oh, the games we play with faith and trust,
and projecting our beliefs into the world!

Oooommmmm

There's a difference between
assuming something is going to happen,
and giving your openhearted
blessing for it to happen,
a difference between working toward a goal,
and working toward a goal
with your heart's full intention.

At first, it is uncomfortable
to have your pride "burned away" —
then, eventually, it can be like a warm breeze
that helps bring you back in sync with
the YOU that you want to be You.

Be the YOU that you *want* to be You!

One of my goals in this life
is to not get stuck in anything.
This makes it easier to keep an awareness
of the bigger picture.

People get upset at being "relationship" alone,
but it is more essential and rare to develop
a true relationship with yourself.

This is where the difference between
being alone and lonely comes in.

Oooommmmm

Be God awe-full in a good way!
Full of awe for the Divine.

Oooommmmm

Dear Lord, let me be in harmony
with Thy Highest Will.

Oooommmmm

You can't always serve God,
move in harmony with spirit,
and also please everyone all the time.

Oooommmmm

Spirituality is always focusing on the God in every situation.

The social structures we humans manufacture are reflections of something much greater, purer, and more phenomenally organized.

For example, our judicial systems may be but a reflection of the great karmic laws of the universe.

Our education systems might be a microcosm of our purpose for being in this world, to learn and grow.

What would be the odds that our first contact "outside our world," would be with beings from the same physical space dimension as our own?

Stop looking to the skies for aliens.

We have always been in relationship
with beings from other realms.

Some move through deep recesses of our minds, others orchestrate general events of humanity. Countless energies, including specific and non-specific intelligence, contribute to this grand dance we call "life."

There is nothing alien about this.
More universes lie on the palm of your hand
than have ever been imagined
in the mind of any human being.

Oooommmmm

Sometimes we learn to make right choices
by seeing how it feels to make wrong choices.

Oooommmmm

I often look at life as research.
Part of the study is to answer
"for what" are we doing this research?

Oooommmmm

Challenges are not necessarily bad,
and having challenges
does *not* necessarily indicate
that someone has bad karmas.

In fact, challenges may be a sign
of a soul who is extra-willing to grow.

Ooommmm

Disharmony.com

Is life too easy?

Come to disharmony.com,
and we'll match you with someone
who will push all your buttons
and give you lots of challenges.

Ooommmm

Disclaimer:
I'm a fairly reclusive monastic lifestyle artist.

Ooommmm

There is only one friend.

Ooommmmm

Just relax,
at least when you
have some peaceful time,
and let everything be as it is.

Ooommmmm

The importance of an apology:
Apologizing takes away karmas.

It's like asking forgiveness from
the God spirit that exists in the other person.

Ooommmmm

We don't have to spend hours
doing research for something,
if we can just open to the right page.

That's one of the magical perks
when we're in the flow.

Ooommmmm

Each scientific discovery can lead to a breaking of the false, egocentric world view. It is in the place where newly discovered knowledge pokes holes in our limited understanding that science meets spirituality, where our intellect meets the sacred.

A lot of people on the spiritual path are "one with God" sometimes — for example, during meditation, or in the company of other lovers of God.

The trick is to be in that greater awareness even while moving through all the facets of our lives. This may require a dual awareness at first, plus a lot of grace.

I welcome God
into every moment of my life.

There are a lot of things I know
that I don't always practice.

But at least I know them.

We all know more than we practice.

Oooommmmm

When you hear spiritual and psychological scholars say that you create this world with your thoughts, it is important to remember and understand that your mind generates many thoughts that may never come to the light of your conscious awareness.

You may pass someone and subconsciously think, "He's a jerk," without even noticing that you think it.

If you notice this kind of subconscious chatter, you could replace those subconscious responses by thinking, "He is divine spirit!" (Or at least that *someone* is divine spirit.)

Oooommmmm

I am a free spirit,
but in my own way,
and not to conform to other people's ideas
of what a free spirit would look like.

Otherwise it wouldn't be free, would it?

Oooommmmm

All the spiritual insights of countless ages:
magical powers, centuries of exploration,
extraordinary revelations of human potential,
all locked away from us
by a thin veil: Memory.

When we assume that our memory potential
is limited to this life,
we forget much.

Oooommmmm

The key to enlightenment
is to get it so you don't forget it.

Oooommmmm

It's possible to interpret
events in real life like dreams.

They can be prophetic,
and have deeper meanings and symbolism.

Oooommmmm

The emotions and thoughts we put out
are like ordering a meal:

- Fear is like sending out an order for what is feared.

- Visioning is like filling out a request form for what you're envisioning.

Uplift your feelings and thoughts,
and you uplift your life

Oooommmmm

Stop being motivated by greed.

Oooommmmm

Leaving this world is like being a worker who is leaving a really tough job that has kept things going financially.

You're leaving to move to a greater place, to a much better job, where you'll have better working conditions, more respect, and lots of unexpected perks.

And yet, the people you work with are just upset to be losing you and your skills from their "world." They get together and mourn your loss as they dress in black and weep.

Some workers make this transition
without even realizing they are
leaving for a great, better job.

Ooommmmm

An important metaphysical law:

Whatever we
focus on becomes strengthened.

Ooommmmm

Understand that wherever you are,
in whatever conditions,
that is your destiny in this world.
Your outer circumstances are only
one small part of who you really are,
which reaches far beyond
the known world and universe.

Oooommmmm

Look for opportunities for prayer
when you read the news,
see photos of missing children,
or hear sounds of ambulances.
Send blessings, and become a clearer
channel for God's blessing.

Oooommmmm

Whatever one person experiences reverberates through the entire web of humanity, especially when many view and think about the event, such as with a media or social media focus.

Oooommmmm

Balance and discernment are necessary.

A Middle Eastern saying says,
"Trust in Allah, but tie your camel."

As I've learned along the way,
if you're not an astute altruist,
you may become a destitute altruist.

If you ever start thinking you're insignificant or unimportant, stop and look at your physical body. Look at all the profound complexity of nature conspiring to keep your body alive, from the unceasing work of your heart and other organs, to molecular functions we haven't even discovered yet.

It is not logical to conclude,
upon contemplating these things,
that you are anything less than phenomenal,
and somehow worth all the effort.

We have these bodies,
but we're the soul, coming and going,
staying for a picnic or two,
or two million.

We are finite and infinite.

Oooommmmm

I will be here however long I am here,
and then I will go.

Oooommmmm

It is beneficial to explore whatever writings and expressions are left from ancient cultures.

Perhaps these "primitive" cultures lagged behind us in terms of technological knowledge, but at the same time, some of their belief systems allowed them entry into understandings and knowledge that would boggle our minds, thrill our spirit, and combine to lead to a grand new understanding of this world.

Oooommmmm

Scientists have described certain qualities
that determine if something is
alive or inanimate.

But in truth, it's all alive.

This entire universal creation
is a living expression
of supreme Consciousness.

Ooooommmmm

Being in the present moment,
has the effect of slowing down time.

Then we can get in there between
the particles of time, and do things.

Ooooommmmm

Change the way you think about things,
and you change the things.

It's not anger – it's ENERGY!

Ooooommmmm

In the soul's journey,
all things happen for a reason.

All flavors of life must be tasted,
and all notes of the flute must be played,
with each individual breath.

Oooommmmm

Treasure Each Moment.

Oooommmmm

Science has discovered that we leave our DNA
everywhere, through skin, saliva, and blood.

This supports the idea that our vibrations
can affect and change what we are near.

DNA carries our particular combination of
vibrations, our energy fingerprint.

Physical DNA sequences are also
physical manifestations of spiritual patterns.

Oooommmmm

Life is a game, and an offering

The universe created mirrors and the quality of reflection, so we could see ourselves. It makes the play more exciting and dramatic.

Visual self-perception also encourages egocentric misconceptions that give the universe so much entertainment through us, with all our dramatic escapades.

People: I'm happy when they come,
and often happy when they go

I'd rather have someone be unfriendly to me,
than friendly for a hidden,
greed-based motive.

Challenges are not necessarily bad,
and having challenges
does *not* necessarily mean
that someone has bad karmas.

In fact, challenges may be a sign of a soul
who is extra-willing to grow.

Oooommmmm

Big tragedies, properly digested, can bring
new awakenings, transformations,
new appreciation, new freshness,
a more tender heart,
courage to rise up to the situation,
self-respect at how you pulled through,
and a deeper connection with God.

Oooommmmm

Everything is scripted by Consciousness:
Scripted, acted, directed, edited, and enjoyed.

Oooommmmm

One example of how Universal Consciousness
communicates with us in our lives can be seen
in how many foods grown on Mother Earth
let us know, consciously or subconsciously,
what health purposes they serve:

Kidney beans help heal kidneys;
walnuts nourish the brain.
Tomatoes with their chambers help the heart.
Celery sticks support bone strength;
and sliced carrots look like the eye's iris.

Learn to discern the rich guidance
woven throughout this creation.

Oooommmmm

Instead of Murphy's law telling you
that what can go wrong will go wrong,
or Occam's razor that looks
for the simplest explanation,
I have Kumuda's law, which says
to imagine the most optimistic possibility.

Oooommmmm

Through the space of quiet mind,
we can access the realm
of silent intuitive knowing.

We can't always integrate what is encountered
in the realm of "silent intuitive knowing"
back into our thinking systems,
because this knowing takes place on
a very different, subtle plane that
doesn't necessarily translate into our usual
physical, psychological, and cultural
frameworks of experience.

Oooommmmm

There is a place that is
neither up nor down, neither in nor out.

That is the source,
from which all blessings flow,
and from which all creation
becomes manifest.

Thou art That.

Oooommmmm

Since we don't know what will happen
after we or someone else dies,
why not go with the theory that
whatever happens is good and
even better than we could imagine
from this bound physical life on earth?

Oooommmmm

May I be a blessing to everyone I see,
and may they be a blessing to me,

Oooommmmm

One way to make our destiny better
is to accept and become content
with our destiny as it already is.

If we only try to change
external circumstances
to satisfy our desires,
we'll never be satisfied,
because desires will always change.

Oooommmmm

A suggestion for the news:

If you report extensively on a story about a man who forgot his baby in the car and came back to find that the baby had died, it would be good to also give educational information, such as statistics on how often this happens and suggestions on how viewers can make sure to always remember the child in their car.

Don't just report disasters,
help to stop them.

Oooommmmm

Being aware is different from being worried.

Oooommmmm

Monopoly taught many generations
the unfortunate idea that
no matter how much you have,
you only win if you have
more than everyone else.

Oooommmmm

Time for a God Bath:

God is so kind and gracious to me.
I feel His love shining on me
like a big shower of light.

I feel Her grace showering down upon me,
holding and supporting me,
and shining out from me.

Grace shines down upon me.
Grace upholds and supports me.
Grace shines out from me.

Ooommmmm

Someone asked if I believe in a God.
Yes, but take out the "a."

Ooommmmm

Trust God,
Trust the Universe,
Trust your own good karma.

Ooommmmm

Purity and goodness of heart
are the best way to look beautiful,
regardless of the configuration
and size of your features.

Oooommmmm

Religion, philosophy and science
are three approaches
toward the same thing:
discovering more about THAT
which defies current human knowledge.

Oooommmmm

The truth doesn't always come
in neat packages.

Oooommmmm

My strongest motivation is
joyful, creative service.

Oooommmmm

For convenience sake, we bathe ourselves in toxins that kill brain cells and weaken our bodies. The disease of egocentricity focuses on immediate convenience, laziness, and surface personal comfort.

If we understood what that bottle
of scrubbing bubbles was doing to us,
we would throw it away.

Egocentricity is the "problem."

Humility is the absence of other qualities,
such as pride, ego, fear, and greed,
qualities that can create hot sands and
stormy clouds over the pure clear space
of Supreme Consciousness.

Burn up your superficial layer of being.

The biggest ego is to think
that we are separate from God.

Oooommmmm

    The feeling of personal responsibility may help to motivate us to improve our efforts, but it can also create shame, fear, grief, or pride. Too much can pull us out of the flow of "nature expressing itself," and make us feel individual, different, and separate from the whole.

Oooommmmm

Part of the game is that we don't get to know
exactly what our task here is.

Oooommmmm

The power in each moment invites us to focus on what we are doing, instead of spending all our energy on what we may do in the future. It's a subtle shift.

Oooommmmm

Eventually, we come to a place,
whether through a spiritual path,
a scientific contemplation,
or a metaphysical understanding of
the nature of the universe,
where we know that ultimately,
all is as it should be.

Then we can stop getting in the way,
as we consciously allow the
false notion of ego-responsibility
and separateness to fall away.

Oooommmmm

God, Let me be humble without having to be
pushed into humility through tragic events.

Oooommmmm

Right now — a part of you is dying,
so the next blossoming
can come forth freely and freshly.

Oooommmmm

As soon as you put your hand
on someone to heal them,
God places His healing hand on you.

Healing grace goes to you
and through you at the same time.

This is one example of how giving
becomes, and simultaneously is, receiving.

Ooommmmm

I tend to meet people where they're at,
which is great
when I'm in good company.

Ooommmmm

Challenging times
can help to break up
and digest your bad karmas,
like a storm creating space for calmness,
or the breakdown before a breakthrough.

Ooommmmm

Mistakes and their negative effects can be difficult and painful, and can bring up feelings of guilt and anger (often toward one's self), but these so called "mistakes" are not necessarily "bad" in an ultimate sense.

Due to mistakes, we may receive deeper understandings, learn new lessons, or find ourselves forced to look at limitations that may have been holding us back.

Mistakes can be a gateway to new growth.

Ooooommmm

Just because someone cooks or gives you something, that doesn't mean you have to eat it. This applies to food and anything else.

Inner guidance comes first.

Ooooommmm

The details don't matter, grace matters.

Ooooommmm

If you have more, enjoy and give.
If you have less, enjoy and conserve
(and still find ways to give).

Oooommmmm

It's not necessarily possible to elevate our consciousness and expect the whole vast field of our personality and experience to hop up to the same space all at once.

This is where we get the ups and downs of the spiritual journey, the power and grace of knowing and trusting our oneness with the universe, contracting down into feeling bad because we forgot to call somebody back.

Eventually, there has to be integration.

Oooommmmm

Okay God, you can make this easy or hard.
My choice is easy,
but Thy Will be done.

Oooommmmm

A powerful method of soul healing
for spiritual and personal evolution
is to know and trust that
everything, everything, and
everything else is the Will of God.

Then we can expand our mental concepts
to grasp what that means
and how it can be.

Oooommmmm

Being "realized" doesn't necessarily mean becoming oblivious to all pain and difficulty. It's not like getting a shot of novocain against the troubles of life, where you are no longer aware of the suffering of this world. It's more like getting laughing gas.

You may still feel the pain or have to see and experience suffering, but you don't hate the pain. You transform it into a different, more uplifting interpretation. You know the pain of "drilling" can heal a bigger pain.

Oooommmmm

When you know
something is your job to do,
it is better to just do it than to
spend a lot of time and energy
requiring that some specific
material benefit must come to you.

Relish the joy of serving and living
in harmony with the flow of nature,
while staying free from attachments
to the results of your actions,
and remaining flexible
to the "Will of God."

Oooommmmm

If only we got paid for all the work
we do while dreaming.

Oooommmmm

Don't limit where wisdom comes from,
or through whom God speaks to you.

Oooommmmm

    Offer blessings for all the trauma taking place around the world right now, along with all the happiness and enjoyments. With so many starving, thirsty, violent, and hungry lives, this planet is drenched in sorrow.

    We could alleviate these sufferings to some degree, however, even those with unimagined riches have sorrow, though they may have the means to temporarily "drown their sorrows" in many luxuries and indulgences.

Oooommmmm

We need a paradigm shift to incorporate
more of our recently discovered scientific,
psychological, and spiritual knowledge
into the world's general view.

Like computer programs,
every now and then,
evolving species have to upgrade
to a better system software.

Oooommmmm

I want to contribute
something amazing to the world,
to help bring light to the world.

Oooommmmm

Sometimes the purpose of difficult times
may be for us to learn to be
more caring, generous, and kind
than those we've encountered.

Oooommmmm

One little bad can sometimes save you
from many big bads.

Oooommmmm

I really like helping other people
achieve their dreams.
Although I did get burned once,
so became more reticent and alert about what
my help might be bringing to the world.

Oooommmmm

Alternate measurements of time allow for many dimensions to co-exist, simultaneously.

We live in the same physical space as a lot of very small and very large alternate dimensional realities.

An entire lifetime for some life forms may be less than a second in human time. And an entire human lifetime is but a drop in the ocean of universal time.

Time is the ultimate universal space-saver.

It's all organized holographically — co-existing, and for the most part unaware of all the other worlds that move within, through, and all around each note of their own musical score within the grand universal symphony.

Those unperceiveable dust mites crawling on our skin right now are the least of what's going on that we don't see.

Oooommmm

When seeing the ruins of the World Trade Center and other destroyed monuments and cities around the world, remember that one day, it's all going to look like that.

Our culture's remnants will eventually be buried by the sands of time, culture upon culture buried like a big societal lasagna, until the day comes when this ball of living clay explodes and is no more.

Find out who you really are.
Do it now.

Oooommmmm

There is a big difference between
knowing you are going to die and
KNOWING YOU ARE GOING TO DIE !!!!!!!!!

Oooommmmm

Each person gets to die one day —
or many days, if you believe in reincarnation.

Oooommmmm

Imagine all the different kinds of death.
Which kind would you choose,
and why?

Quick? Painless? Long illness? Explosion?
Heart stopping? Burned by fire?

Drowned in water? Buried under the earth?

Peacefully, in your sleep?

At the happiest moment of your life?

In the depths of despair,
when you're relieved to be getting out?

In the middle of holy communion with spirit?

A helpful TIP
from the Bhagavad Gita:

Think of the highest during your
last moment of life —
think of the Eternal Spirit of God!

Oooommmm

God said through inner guidance:
I want you to have no preference
whether to stay or go from this world.

Then you will truly be able to serve and
attain that which you truly seek
(even if you don't quite know with your mind
what it is that you truly seek).

Oooommmmm

Spirituality is not one path fits all.

Oooommmmm

The more blessings we give to the world,
through more and more avenues — to more
people, or more fully to the same people —
the more our personal energy conduit
to the infinite universal life force grows
to accommodate the greater amount
of light-grace that is flowing
through us into the world.

Oooommmmm

Sometimes, it's better not to have too much *jnana*, worldly knowledge, about spiritual matters we really want to know, so that limited knowledge doesn't obscure our view of *vijnana*, the wisdom of deeper knowing.

Sometimes too much book learning
can obscure higher truths from our view.

Jokes are only funny
to those who get them.

So it is with the Cosmic Joke
that laughs and chuckles through it all.

Being happy all the time
doesn't necessarily mean
you have to look happy all the time.

I'm not always happy,
but I know there's a part of me
that's always happy.

Oooommmmm

In our journey toward perfection,
that perfection already is.

Oooommmmm

You know that bit of time in the early morning when you first wake up and are self-aware, but haven't yet remembered all the circumstances of your life, such as who you are, where you live, what you do, what you have, what you did yesterday and what you have to do tomorrow?

That space of unadulterated consciousnesss
is the Self.

That is being in the now.

Oooommmmm

One thing I've learned from the birds who come to my gazebo-shaped bird feeder is that when they go a day or two without seeds after being regularly fed, they become very focused on what they're doing, quietly eating and fitting peacefully together, with some collecting seeds on the ground, and others flying back and forth around the feeder.

But when the feeder stays full for a long time, they'll start noticing the birds around them and chasing them away from the feeder in an aggressive manner that you wouldn't expect from such gentle looking creatures.

Human beings can be like this too.
Sometimes a bit of scarcity
helps us be more focused and humble.

Walking away can sometimes be
the greatest act of compassion
for everyone involved.

The life of a mosquito lasts around 10 days; the life of a human being, perhaps 100 years.

The ancient *Vedas* of India describe other levels of beings — call them gods, angels, guides, or parallel universes — that experience longer time frames than we do: hundreds, thousands, millions or more of our human years.

Oooommmmm

This moment right now is eternal.
Every moment is eternal.

Oooommmmm

One day for our mother earth may be relative to thousands of centuries of human time.

A perceiver watching the earth from a faster subjective time might see the cyclical creation and destruction of various species of life as occurring quickly, according to a biological pattern we are unable to see from our smaller time frames.

Oooommmmm

When you're steeped in spiritual wisdom and awareness, there is no need for, "My God is better than your God," because you are in touch with the real God that exists behind all the outer symbolic representations of that formless God that ultimately expresses as and beyond everything that is knowable and unknowable.

Oooommmmm

We draw to us what we resonate with.
Natural laws keep away whatever doesn't fit into our bandwidth of experience.

Oooommmmm

There are certain things you may not
want to talk about with people who aren't
on a similar level of consciousness.
Their lack of ability to understand
your more subtle understandings, and
the resulting misinterpretations, can possibly
bring your awareness down in some ways.

Oooommmmm

Sometimes, it's good to be
an undefined or indefinable entity.

Oooommmmm

One challenge is to become less egocentric from the space of egocentricity.

Our judgment of what is or isn't moving toward or away from egocentricity is tainted by our egocentric concepts and notions, which are not accurate or complex enough to understand what is really going on.

Oooommmmm

We get lazy.

There is surface lazy and there is deep lazy.

Many very busy people are deep lazy. In fact, keeping very busy is one of the favorite methods a "deep lazy person" uses to keep from having to contemplate what is really happening here.

Oooommmmm

One of the great challenges in life is to
stay true to the best of what exists inside of us.

Others can either help to raise us up into
greater levels of awareness, or they can keep us
limited to their small views of who and what
they think we are or should be.

In quiet and peaceful solitude,
I find it much easier to remember
my deeper wisdom, aspirations, and priorities,
without getting as easily swept away
by the desires and concepts of others.

Oooommmmm

Once we learn the power of words, we don't
let ourselves say things like, "he makes me sick,"
because we have respect for the power of the
words that move through us.

We know that everything we say
is a command to the universe.

Oooommmmm

Words are what keep us
bound to time and space.

Words are our best friend
and our worst enemy.

Words are like the cells of our bodies,
emitting the free radicals
that destroy our youth,
even as they maintain our lives.

Ooommmmm

Here's a deal I made with God:

I'm going to do things that I want to do.

So all You have to do is make me
want to do what You want me to do.

I'll stay open to Your guidance
on what I should do and want to do.

Much easier than pushing at every turn!

Ooommmmm

Let's say that our space program gets it together enough to land on an inhabited planet in another solar system.

Imagine that we land on this planet and find beings similar in intellectual evolution to human beings.

Let's say we find that a small percentage of the planet lives in opulence, with electronic representations of untold amounts of currency sitting unneeded and unused in bank accounts, while the rest of beings living on that planet suffer and starve.
What would we think
of such a planet and species?

Oooommmmm

Our knowledge of the universe
should be expanding every time
there is a new technological invention,
and with every significant event
available for us to explore.

Oooommmmm

Hasn't anyone considered that maybe
the earth actually makes some use of the
oils we've been pulling out of the ground?

Nature usually puts things there
for a reason.

Oooommmmm

I have a karmic "force field" around me
for people who can't enter
my particular combination of
consciousness levels, energy frequencies,
world view, or life vision.

We all do.
This is one way our thoughts
Create our world.

Oooommmmm

We are like silly putty –
whatever we press against,
we begin to look like.

Oooommmmm

The same people who can
be most uplifting for you at one time,
can at another time become very un-uplifting,
either due to their changes, to your changes,
or to a combination of changes.

I have a friendship with God,
and no other human relationship
or friendship comes close.

Human friends come and go, but
God is always there, always dependable.
So make friends with God.

God is in my life
God is my life
God is life
God IS
God
IS

A thought may be
coming from divine guidance, if it:

- Comes as a flash of inspiration
- Makes good sense and is helpful
- Comes with good omens, including small or large miracles that may represent a universal confirmation of the guidance

Oooommmmm

There are no good numbers or bad numbers.
Every number has its place.

Oooommmmm

When you're spiritually awakened, it can be helpful to be around other spiritually awakened people — people, for example, who can look at a challenge in your life and dig with you to find the spiritual aspect, the guiding lesson, and the holy blessing "rose" hidden beneath the thorns.

Oooommmmm

Are we here to worship the bowl,
or that which is carried in the bowl?
If the bowl becomes empty,
or filled with something unhealthy,
do we keep drinking from it
just because that bowl
had previously
served great
nectar?

Oooommmm

My artist nature loves to express
what my mind, heart, and soul have tasted.

Oooommmm

Sometimes it is the quietest times
that allow us to hear the "voice of God,"
the wisdom that speaks at all times
to and through us, but softly,
and often obscured by all the internal
and external noises of day-to-day life.

Oooommmm

If a tragedy comes along that makes you
loosen your dependence
on the smaller safety
and discover a bigger safety,
then that so-called tragedy is also a blessing.

Oooommmmm

Dip into conscious remembrance of God now,
without being told that
you've just lost a loved one,
without finding out that you have
two months to live.

Oooommmmm

I offered myself to write
Spirituality For Dummies, and God said "Yes."

And when God says "Yes," everyone says
"Yes" (including the agent and publisher).

It's the ultimate dictatorship, because
God lives in and as all things.

Oooommmmm

Dear God,

Bless me to always remember you,
without having to be
driven to remembrance
by tragedy.

In the Bhakti Yoga of devotion,
we focus all our energy toward a single object.

When the object is removed, that energy has no place to go but back into ourselves.

One lesson from this reality television, news-obsessed time in human evolution and cognitive development is to realize how interesting regular old life is — especially if you have the best journalists, politicians, comedians, and other professionals milking every drop of the event (any event) for nearly 24 hours a day.

It's beneficial to be able to
handle dichotomies, co-existing opposites.

This is the only way to be able to accept the dichotomy that we are one with God, the divine, and yet still experience our lives and lessons on this earth plane.

Oooommmmm

We are this personality, this limited being,
and yet we are not.

We are a wave and a particle
at the same time.

Oooommmmm

Some get to go through
their karmic tests in luxury.
This is a type of "good karma," when we
get to learn the lessons and go through
our karmas in pleasant circumstances.
Same tests, but a more comfortable road.

Oooommmmm

Each person can sense the unfathomable
potential that exists inside of them.

Every child knows they are a child of God.

They may or may not use the word God
to describe their relationship to this universe
that has brought them forth, but they know.

Beneath all quests for knowledge,
there must be an understanding

— spoken or unspoken —

that what is being discovered and described
is but a tiny ray of That Which Is.

Just because it is time
to start doing something differently,
doesn't mean you shouldn't have been
doing it the way you were.

Anything that gets you
completely focused in the present moment
can bring a spiritual experience.

Present moment focus can clear a path
through debris in your mind.

Rumi described it as
a gust of wind that clears the eyes.

Oooommmmm

One reason why being in the present moment
is so important is that when we
do things in the present moment

— spontaneously —

our actions are naturally in harmony with
the universal "fingerprint" of that moment.

Oooommmmm

I intentionally offer my self,
my life, all that I am
and all that I am not, to YOU.

Oooommmmm

May your body be healthy,
May your pockets be wealthy.
May good news knock
upon your door,
And may God bless you forever more.

Find more things that
make you go

Ooommmm

on the
Night Lotus Website:

www.nightlotus.com

www.ingramcontent.com/pod-product-compliance
Lightning Source LLC
Chambersburg PA
CBHW020933090426
42736CB00010B/1121